Dear —
This [is] [something] [you] might
get a smile from!

As 94 comes to a close, I
think of all I've been
through these last two
years and how you were
always there for me. You'll
never know how much you
mean to me — you've been
such a true friend.

I'll always be here
for you too —

Sabrina

THE
SINGLE
Woman's
ALMANAC

By Suzanne Brown, Kim Dodd,
and Lisa Steadman

Designed by Michel Design

PETER PAUPER PRESS, INC.
WHITE PLAINS · NEW YORK

Copyright © 1992
Peter Pauper Press, Inc.
202 Mamaroneck Avenue
White Plains, NY 10601
All rights reserved
ISBN 0-88088-502-5
Printed in Hong Kong
7 6 5 4 3 2 1

THE
SINGLE
Woman's
ALMANAC

JANUARY

● ● ● ●

January 1

New Year's Resolution #23: Promise yourself to celebrate being a single, independent woman.

January 3

Get yourself a manicure. You can't rule the world with chipped nails.

January 4

Reread *Gone With the Wind*. What was Scarlett thinking? You'd take Rhett *or* Ashley!

January 5

Find out that there's a 7 to 1 ratio of men to women at Vail. Decide to learn how to ski.

January 6

Brownies and a Diet Coke for dinner. You've covered the four basic food groups—sugar, chocolate, caffeine, and carbonation!

January 7

Your boss takes you out for lunch. Think of the money saved and the time off from work.

January 8

Have dinner with your sister Debbie and her husband Michael. You wish you could find a guy as great as Michael.

January 9

Meet your new neighbor Steve by the mailboxes. He may be someone to keep your eye on!

January 10

Celebrate! You finally figured out how to tape something on your VCR when you're not home.

January 11

Subscribe to *Road and Track.* Plan to buy a new car, and it won't hurt your blind date conversation either!

January 12

Give your teddy bear a hug—he's faithful.

January 13

Blind date with Lester—hope he's cuter than his name.

January 14

Depressed over last night's lousy date. At least he paid for dinner.

January 15

Visit the museum and get your fix of ancient Greek statues. You haven't seen such toned bodies in a while!

January 16

Stay late at work discussing a marketing strategy with a colleague. Accomplish a great deal, and get a free cab ride home on the company!

January 18

Your friends Lea and Evan are getting married! Oh God, you're a bridesmaid again.

January 19

Eat triple fudge nut ice cream right out of the carton. Who will know?

January 20

Rent the movie *Notorious*. Cary Grant is your date tonight.

January 21

Concentrate on climbing to the top of the corporate ladder. Be glad there's no guy around to distract you.

January 22

Babysit for Danny, Debbie and Michael's five-year-old. Begin his sensitivity training young!

January 23

Borrow a cup of sugar from your cute neighbor Steve. Bring over home-baked chocolate chip cookies to say thank you.

January 25

Gossip with your girlfriend on the phone into the wee hours of the night.

January 26

Your cholesterol is plunging! Isn't it great not to have a "steak and potatoes" man around?

January 28

Go out to dinner with your friend Joyce and her husband. Doesn't she ever go anywhere without him?

January 29

Wish that your favorite department store was open on Saturday night—then you would never need a date!

January 30

Your birthday's coming up. Start thinking of ways to drop subtle hints to your friends and loved ones.

January 31

Pluck your eyebrows. Are bushy or thin brows in this year?

FEBRUARY

▲ ▲ ▲ ▲

February 1

Buy your favorite magazines with good horoscopes. Hey, this month looks out of this world!

February 2

Rent the movie *Crossing Delancey* and wonder if the pickle man is your destiny.

February 3

It's been a real dating dry spell. Should you consider video dating?

February 4

Girls' night out!

February 5

Hook up your new stereo unassisted.
Who needs men?

February 6

Cook a beautiful meal all by yourself and
eat it from your best china.

February 7

Take 5-year-old Danny to the department
store and teach him to wait outside the
dressing room.

February 8

Go out on reasonably nice blind date
with Joe. Somehow, though, you just
can't picture having his children.

February 9

See cute fireman. Consider setting your
kitchen on fire.

February 10

Order pizza in—with extra onions and garlic!

February 11

Buy fresh flowers at the corner store. Put a little Spring in your life!

February 12

Let the lady at the cosmetics counter give you a make-over. Buy $100 worth of makeup to keep that natural look!

February 13

Appreciate that the toilet seat is always down!

February 14

Valentine's Day. Dress in black.

February 16

Order in Szechuan chicken. Your fortune cookie predicts a love-filled future. You wish the "future" would hurry up already.

February 17

Give up ice cream. It's fattening.

February 18

Sunday morning. Isn't it great not to have to fight over the crossword?

February 19

Sign up for a massage, close your eyes, and let someone rub your stress away.

February 20

Babysit for your nephew Danny again. Tell him it's okay to cry.

February 21

Wake up alone at 4 A.M. Order a new sweater from your favorite mail order catalog.

February 22

Wear sexy lingerie under your clothes. You're a *femme fatale* even if no one else knows.

February 23

Your best friend calls you crying in the middle of the night because her boyfriend dumped her. At least no one is around to dump you.

February 24

Treat yourself to Haagen-Dasz. Ice cream ban suspended. It's been a tough week.

February 25

Screen your calls and hope Lester gets the hint!

February 26

Go see that show everyone's been talking about with your best friend Julie.

February 27

Help Steve, the cute neighbor, with his laundry. You never knew separating colors could be so much fun.

February 28

Subscribe to *Alaskan Men* magazine. So many Northern hunks looking for dates! Decide you can deal with 50° below zero temperature.

MARCH

March 1

Turn down blind date suggested by your grandmother. Remember Lester?

March 2

Curl up in bed with *People* magazine. It's the "Sexiest Man Alive" issue.

March 3

Bake brownies, but eat half the batter before it hits the pan!

March 4

Go to your engaged friend Lea's bridal shower. Covet her new microwave.

March 5

Work up the courage to go out to dinner by yourself. It isn't hard to be brave when the restaurant has good-looking waiters.

March 6

There's a Gary Cooper film festival. Looks like you have plans for the rest of the week.

March 7

Sent on a business trip to a hot tropical climate. These perks are perky.

March 10

Join a reading group. Do you think Danielle Steele will make it to the reading list?

March 11

Check out the local flea market. Maybe antiques won't be the only find!

March 12

Treat yourself to cappuccino, and people-watch in style.

March 13

Go shopping with your mother. It's as much fun as ever—she still pays for everything.

March 14

Reading group meets tonight. It's at Lea's; you can put off cleaning your apartment for another week.

March 15

Get great hair cut. Feel in control of
your life.

March 16

Take the bus across town. Give your seat
to an elderly person. You may want
someone to do it for you some day!

March 17

Browse through the late-night bookstore.
Buy two novels even though you already
have a stack by your bed.

March 18

Stock up on hosiery. You can never have
too many pairs of nylons.

March 19

Have a heated political discussion with
Debbie and Michael. When did they get
so conservative?

March 20

Take your little nephew Danny to the
florist. Show him the superiority of long-
stemmed roses to daisies!

March 21

First day of Spring. Time to get into
shape—again.

March 22

Impress your boss with the presentation
you've been preparing all month.
Brownie points are better than brownies.

March 23

They can't live without you. Ask for that
raise.

March 24

Got promoted. Who knows where the ladder of success will end?

March 25

Spend your bonus on a new TV.

March 26

Come home late from work. Forget nutrition, and zap yourself a frozen dinner in the microwave.

March 27

Write a letter to the editor of the local newspaper. There's no reason you should sit back when you've got something to say.

March 28

Brush up on your Italian. You never know when the language of love will come in handy.

March 29

Decide to call your married friend, Joyce. Whoops, it's past 9 P.M.—too late to call married people.

March 30

It's Oscar Night. You haven't had that many good-looking men in your living room in a long time.

March 31

The business cards with your new title are ready. Send one to your mother. You've come a long way, baby!

APRIL

April 1

Tell your mother that you're engaged.
April Fool!

April 2

Easter's right around the corner. Buy
yourself a big stuffed bunny to keep you
company.

April 3

Lea and Evan are having their
engagement party this week.
Shop for the perfect dress. You have to
look spectacular—it's your first chance to
scope the ushers.

April 4

Daylight Savings Time is around the corner. Aren't you glad you can start jogging in the park after work again?

April 5

Meet Doug, one of Evan's ushers, at the engagement party. This is one wedding you won't mind being in!

April 6

Call Lea to get the scoop on Doug. He's available!

April 7

Finally buy that hat you keep trying on. Pretend you're Audrey Hepburn.

April 8

Cook dinner for your best friend Julie from that recipe you've been saving. Stay up 'til midnight giggling.

April 9

Earth Day is coming up. Plan on going to the rally in the park to show your support.

April 10

Go shopping for a full-length mirror. Buy the one that makes you look five pounds thinner.

April 11

Buy a lottery ticket. It just may be your lucky day.

April 12

Do your taxes on your own. You're getting a refund and saving an accountant's fee.

April 13

Oh, no, your good friend Karen is being transferred 2,000 miles away for work. What are you going to do without her?

April 14

You cried during the latest telephone commercial, you binged on chocolate, and you hung up on your mother. It must be PMS.

April 15

It's two days before your period. You're so bloated you could float to work!

April 16

It's a big weekend. You and Julie are hitting all the factory outlets.

April 17

Rally from your depression about Karen moving away. Have a fabulous going-away party for her. Everyone thinks you're a terrific hostess!

April 18

Run into your cute neighbor Steve in the laundry room. Whoops, your black teddie just happens to fall at his feet.

April 19

Buy hot dress. Your old boyfriend will be at this weekend's party.

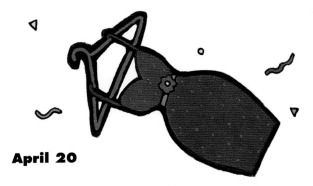

April 20

Talk all night on the phone with your best friend discussing accessories for your dress.

April 21

Walk for your favorite charity. Get all your friends to sponsor you, and it's terrific exercise.

April 22

Your division goes out for dinner. It's a good opportunity to mix business with pleasure.

April 23

Recycle your soda cans. Every little bit counts.

April 24

Your bathroom needs scrubbing. Looks like you've got a date with Mr. Clean.

April 25

Power lunch with potential new client. You're as smooth as the béarnaise sauce.

April 26

Reread some of your favorite old classics. There's nothing like *Wuthering Heights* on a rainy day.

April 28

Dinner with your college friend, Sam. He's having as much trouble finding a woman as you are finding a man.

April 30

Buy yourself a tin of your favorite caviar at the gourmet shop. Be a hedonist, and eat it all at once.

MAY

May 1

Hurray, hurray, the first of May. Outdoor necking starts today!

May 2

Buy yourself a ficus tree. Who says the only life form in your apartment has to be human?

May 3

Wonder how you would describe yourself in a personals ad.

May 4

Mother's Day is coming up. Plan a special day with your Mom.

May 5

Think about joining a health club. Bikini
season right around the corner.

May 6

Karen calls long-distance. She's lonely.
You promise to talk once a week.

May 7

Teach your nephew Danny how to make
a peanut butter and jelly sandwich. Yes,
Danny, real men cook!

May 8

Volunteer to work at the local hospital. It
makes you feel good to be of service.

May 9

Buy trendy work-out clothes in
anticipation of joining health club.

May 10

Buy yourself a real hammer and throw
away your miniature tool kit.

May 11

Join high-tech health club.

May 12

Another blind date set up by your co-worker. Does he really think all beige looks good?

May 13

Receive CPR from cute aerobics instructor after you collapse during your first class.

May 14

Offer to walk Rover, your friend Tina's Saint Bernard. You heard it was a good way to meet men.

May 15

Put off going to the health club. You're sore, and it wouldn't be a good idea to push it.

May 16

Think about going to the health club. Decide that muscles are only sexy on Madonna.

May 17

Lea and Evan have their rehearsal dinner. You and Doug make significant eye contact over the filet mignon and champagne.

May 18

It's the big day for Lea and Evan. You hope Doug can distinguish you from the other seven bridesmaids.

May 19

Sleep in. You and Doug danced the night away at the wedding.

May 20

You call Karen long distance to check in on her. She just bought a new pull-out couch, and your name is written all over it.

May 21

Have dinner at McDonald's. You love a man who's not afraid of wearing a clown suit.

May 22

You don't feel like doing your laundry. Go buy another pair of underwear.

May 23

Go nuts! Have a frozen yogurt with a topping.

May 24

Finally put your photo album together. Edit out the pictures of your old boyfriends.

May 25

The IRS finally sends your refund check. What's it going to be? A share in a beach house or some shares in that biotech firm you heard about?

May 26

Biotech firm went under before you could call your broker. It looks like it's the beach this summer.

May 27

Dinner with the Colonel at Kentucky Fried Chicken. There's nothing like a man in uniform.

May 28

Refinish that antique chair you found at the flea market. You knew watching all those "home improvement" shows would come in handy.

May 29

Give yourself a mud mask and a deep hair conditioning. Hope Steve doesn't stop by for sugar!

May 30

Tutor English at the local high school. It's great to help out, and it's fun to read your old favorites.

May 31

Things are getting out of focus. Is the world spinning faster or do you need glasses?

JUNE

◆ ◆ ◆ ◆

June 1

It's off to the optician. Lucky you aren't being graded on your eye chart test!

June 2

Contacts or glasses? Contacts or glasses? Choose some funky specs and go for the intellectual look.

June 3

The V.P. compliments you on your memo. It's nice to be appreciated.

June 4

There's a message on your answering machine. Doug wants to know if you're free for dinner.

June 5

Cancel health club membership. Exercise is just a fad, anyway.

June 6

Spend a couple of hours on the phone with your best friend Julie deciding what to wear out to dinner with Doug. He's never seen you in casual clothes.

June 7

Attend your college roommate's wedding —another single friend bites the dust.

June 8

Run into your cute neighbor Steve as you're walking out with Doug. Was that a crestfallen look on Steve's face?

June 9

Contemplate last night's dinner with Doug. When you were tipsy at the wedding, you didn't notice how much Doug liked to talk about himself.

June 10

Doug calls to thank you for having dinner with him. Doesn't he know he's not supposed to act like he's so interested?

June 11

Father's Day is approaching. Skip creativity this year, and just buy Dad a tie.

June 12

Give Doug a second chance. Go to the movies. At least he can't talk about himself the whole time.

June 13

You're a bridesmaid—again.

June 14

Another ugly bridesmaid's dress hangs in the closet.

June 15

Screen your calls. "Doug the Dud" hasn't been getting the hint.

June 16

It's your first weekend at the beach. Bring heavy sunscreen. You don't want to be old before your time.

June 17

Get caught in the riptide, but don't worry. The sexy lifeguard has his eye on you. Hmmm, maybe it's time to start something with a younger man.

June 18

An army reserve officer tries to pick you up on the train. He's good-looking—if you like a man in camouflage.

June 19

Take your nephew Danny to the jeweler's. Show him how sparkly the two-carat diamond is compared to a single carat.

June 20

Attend your cousin Lois's wedding. Hide in bathroom when it's time for her to throw the bouquet.

June 21

Sign up for the volleyball league—meet guys, get tan, learn to serve!

June 22

Reorganize your closet. Discover that your old jeans, once too tight, now fit!

June 23

Smile. It's a sunny day, and you feel great!

June 24

Go see a local theater production of *Romeo and Juliet*. Steve, Steve, wherefore art thou, Steve?

June 25

Get highlights put in your hair. A little color goes a long way.

June 26

Order a whopping meal at the local fast food joint and a diet soda—as if that's going to make a difference.

June 27

Paint your apartment. You can choose any color in the rainbow! You have no one to please but yourself.

June 28

Hooray! Two weeks with perfect skin.

June 29

Renew your newspaper subscription, and
cancel the pay-cable stations. How many
old movies can you watch anyway?

June 30

Write to your Congressperson about the
state of the environment. Who says one
voice can't make a difference?

JULY

July 1

Give blood. You've got a spare pint.

July 2

Plan weekend at the beach, and schedule
another hated bikini wax in advance.

July 3

Bonfire at the beach. Everyone looks
good by firelight!

July 4

You don't need a guy to see fireworks!

July 5

Play doubles tennis with your fun
housemate. Oooh, it's a love match.

July 6

Go to the hardware store. Shoo away all the salesmen. You know a Phillips screw driver when you see one.

July 7

You need a vacation. Time to use your frequent flier miles and visit Karen.

July 8

Rent *Roman Holiday*. You don't mind sharing Gregory Peck with Audrey.

July 9

Go out to dinner with the newlyweds, Lea and Evan. Was it your imagination, or were you invisible?

July 10

Give yourself a pedicure. Even your toes need a little attention.

July 11

Break open a box of chocolates. Bite into each piece in search of the best filling.

July 12

Teach yourself a new computer program.
There's nothing like conquering the latest
technology.

July 13

Marketing research project at the library.
Aren't you glad you remember how to
use the microfiche?

July 14

Cook dinner for yourself. You'll wash and
you'll dry—next week!

July 15

Spend Sunday afternoon cooking your
famous spaghetti sauce. Freeze it in small
containers to eat at a later date.

July 16

Subscribe to *Consumer Reports*. It's your money you're spending. Why should you be ignorant about how you're spending it?

July 17

Just found a company checkbook error. Balance is now up $100,000. What shall you suggest they do with it?

July 18

Balanced your checkbook on the first try. You're on a roll.

July 19

Thinking about taking up photography. Who knows what could develop?

July 20

On your way to a black tie party, you meet Steve in the lobby. He walks into the wall. Your new little black dress sure was worth it!

July 21

Spend the whole day on the phone with Julie, analyzing Steve's walking into the wall.

July 22

You've been called for jury duty. Attractive lawyers, distinguished judges, flirty fellow jurors—so many choices, so little time.

July 23

Go for happy hour after work. Remember how much fun your office mates can be after hours.

July 24

Lounge in sweats all day. Who cares? No one's around to see you anyway!

July 26

It's a single woman's double feature bonanza—*The Way We Were* and *Now, Voyager*. What guy would stand for it?

AUGUST

August 3

Go to the movies alone. You don't have to share your Raisinets!

August 4

You're off to visit Karen. Be nice to the chatty woman sitting next to you on the plane—she might have a cute nephew.

August 5

You didn't know how much you missed Karen until you saw her.

August 6

Think about going sightseeing, but
decide to hit all the local boutiques
instead. Some things never change!

August 7

Go out for Sunday brunch with some of
Karen's new friends. It's great how she's
making it on her own in a new town.

August 8

Home from your trip. There are six
messages on your machine. Too bad
they're all from your mother.

August 15

Fix your dripping faucet all by yourself.
You're a woman of the '90's!

August 17

Take a bubble bath and read a trashy novel. You deserve a break today.

August 20

The "Victoria's Secret" catalog arrives. Order yourself a silk robe so you can lounge around in style. You never know when Steve might stop by.

August 24

Get a facial. Feel in control of your skin.

SEPTEMBER

▲ ▲ ▲ ▲ ▲

September 3

Think about taking a course at the nearby college. Which will be best for meeting men—auto mechanics or wine tasting?

September 5

Go to Danny's sixth birthday party. Thank God none of those screaming toddlers are yours!

September 10

Open the door to get your newspaper just as Steve is getting his. Aren't you glad you ordered that sexy "Victoria's Secret" robe, and doesn't he look hot in his boxers?

September 12

You've been promoted to head of your department. You've got your eye on that corner office.

September 13

Now that you've got your promotion, it's time to treat yourself to that new power suit.

September 15

Buy an artsy poster for your pad. Who's around to criticize your taste?

September 21

Autumn's here. Time to pull your sweaters out of mothballs.

September 22

Shop all day Sunday. Ah, the joys of being single!

September 24

Give yourself a day of beauty at the neighborhood salon. Decide you could be a model after all!

September 27

You've got a cold. Where's your mommy when you need her?

September 28

Play touch football in the park. Meet men and get rid of aggression at the same time!

September 29

Join the football pool in the office. You don't know much about sports, so make your selections based on the teams with the tightest ends!

OCTOBER

October 2

Take out the garbage by yourself. Hmm, men do have their uses.

October 3

Blind date with Frank. Being described as "funny and smart" actually meant "good personality," which meant he was "bald and overweight."

October 5

Rent rollerblades for the first time. Thank heaven no one is around to watch you fall!

October 7

Take yourself bike-riding to see the fall foliage.

October 9

Get your hair cut. Is it your imagination, or is every gorgeous man on the street checking you out?

October 11

Rent *Private Benjamin*. If Goldie Hawn doesn't need a man, neither do you.

October 13

Friday night in. Get psyched to rent the latest Kevin Costner movie.

October 14

Babysit for Danny. Introduce him to quiche.

October 16

Have your blind date come up and fix
your broken VCR. He can't kiss, but at
least you save some money on repairs.

October 18

Order in Chinese food. You never get
tired of Lo Mein.

October 21

Invite Steve over to watch *Body Heat* on
your newly repaired VCR!

October 22

Visit the museum and look at the
marvelous French sculpture. Maybe it's
time for a trip to Europe to see Rodin's
The Kiss in person.

October 24

Buy yourself a very expensive pair of black flats—you're worth it.

October 29

Buy a pumpkin and candy for all the neighborhood kids. Just think, all those little boys will be single men one day!

October 31

Dress up for Halloween party.
Go as a bride.

NOVEMBER

November 1

The elections are gearing up. Read all the candidates' literature. It's time to make a thoughtful selection, based on the platforms, not on the tabloids.

November 8

Sign up for ballroom dancing classes. You never know when your Fred Astaire will sweep you up off your feet.

November 9

Girls' night out—decide together that you don't need men anyway.

November 10

Your high school reunion is next week. Your first love is single again. Maybe it's time to reignite the flame!

November 11

Take Danny apple-picking. Tell him Eve
was framed.

November 19

It's the night before your high school
reunion. Should you go for the "casual
but cool" look or should you go dressed
to kill?

November 20

Go to the reunion. Your old flame never
showed, but Greg the Geek turned into
Greg the Gorgeous!

November 21

Bask in the afterglow of the reunion—the
prom queen brought her Slimfast shakes!

DECEMBER

December 2

> *Cosmopolitan* magazine's "Stargazer" hits the stands. Maybe next year holds your one true love!

December 3

> It's the holiday season. Start planning who you're going to trap under the mistletoe.

December 8

Your best friend Julie is having her annual dinner party. Great! You'll have a chance to wear your stunning black velvet dress.

December 11

The holiday season is super, but the prospects for New Year's Eve are beginning to haunt you.

December 12

Surprise snow storm. Show Danny how to make angels in the snow.

December 17

Your office is having a Christmas party. You'll finally find out if that sales rep you talk to on the phone all the time has a face to match his sexy voice.

December 18

Looks like New Year's Eve is taken care of. Lea and Evan are having a blowout party.

December 21

Buy flannel pajamas. It's all that's going to keep you warm this winter.

December 22

Hallelujah! Steve comes over on the pretext of borrowing sugar and asks you out for New Year's Eve.

December 27

Isn't it nice you don't have to shave your legs for three months!

December 31

Moments before Midnight, Steve confesses he's had a crush on you since he moved in. You're starting the new year off with a bang!